The Oriental Institute of The University of Chicago is among the leaders in the recovery of the history, languages and cultures of the ancient Near East. In the halcyon days of the 1930s, when universities and museums conducted expeditions on a scale now unheard of, Oriental Institute teams worked in every country of the Near East. An integral part of each excavation was the expedition photographer, who was entrusted with capturing not only the routine of each day's work but also the moments of discovery and exploration. These images recount some of these memorable moments, as the Oriental Institute sifted the sands of time.

The archive of the Oriental Institute contains over 100,000 negatives documenting the Institute's activities from 1892 to the present. These images record now-vanished temples and tombs, famed archaeologists standing proudly near their greatest finds and scenes of life now effaced by modern times.

Inset photo: James Henry Breasted, founder of the Oriental Institute, at the temple of Amada, Nubia, October 1906

Sifting the Sands of Time

Abu Simbel, Egypt: Nubian on colossal statues on the
facade of the temple of Ramesses II, 1905–1906

Pomegranate, Box 6099, Rohnert Park, CA 94927

Sifting the Sands of Time

Abu Simbel, Egypt: Documenting the battle reliefs of
Ramesses II at Abu Simbel, 1905–1906

Pomegranate, Box 6099, Rohnert Park, CA 94927

Sifting the Sands of Time

Sakkara, Egypt: The Sakkara Expedition copying
inscriptions in the Mastaba of Mereruka, c. 1934

Pomegranate, Box 6099, Rohnert Park, CA 94927

Sifting the Sands of Time

Sakkara, Egypt: Photographing scenes in the tomb of
Mereruka at Sakkara, c. 1934

Pomegranate, Box 6099, Rohnert Park, CA 94927

Sifting the Sands of Time

Sakkara, Egypt: Copying inscriptions on a false door in
the Mastaba tomb of Mereruka, c. 1934

Pomegranate, Box 6099, Rohnert Park, CA 94927

Sifting the Sands of Time

Wadi Halfa, Egypt: University of Chicago professor
copying an inscription, January 1906

Pomegranate, Box 6099, Rohnert Park, CA 94927

Sifting the Sands of Time

Khorsabad, Iraq: Excavation of the gateway of the
citadel of King Sargon II, 1933–1934

Pomegranate, Box 6099, Rohnert Park, CA 94927

Sifting the Sands of Time

Khorsabad, Iraq: Excavation of the gateway of the
citadel of King Sargon II, 1933–1934

Pomegranate, Box 6099, Rohnert Park, CA 94927

Sifting the Sands of Time

Tell Asmar, Iraq: Workman of the Iraq Expedition
examining Sumerian statues, January 1934

Pomegranate, Box 6099, Rohnert Park, CA 94927

Sifting the Sands of Time

Jerwan, Iraq: The Iraq Expedition at the excavation of
the aqueduct of Sennacherib, 1933

Pomegranate, Box 6099, Rohnert Park, CA 94927

Sifting the Sands of Time

Cairo, Egypt: John Hartman photographing
hieroglyphic inscriptions on coffins in the Egyptian
Museum, 1922–1923

Pomegranate, Box 6099, Rohnert Park, CA 94927

Sifting the Sands of Time

Cairo, Egypt: Copying coffin texts in the Egyptian
Museum, 1923

Pomegranate, Box 6099, Rohnert Park, CA 94927

Sifting the Sands of Time

Soleb, Sudan: Epigrapher copying inscriptions on the
doorway of the temple of Amenhotep III at Soleb,
Nubia, 1906–1907

Pomegranate, Box 6099, Rohnert Park, CA 94927

Sifting the Sands of Time

Meroe, Sudan: View of the royal tombs at Meroe,
Nubia, 1906–1907

Pomegranate, Box 6099, Rohnert Park, CA 94927

Sifting the Sands of Time

Meroe, Sudan: Pyramid tomb of Nubian King
Tarekeniwal, 1906-1907

Pomegranate, Box 6099, Rohnert Park, CA 94927

Sifting the Sands of Time

Persepolis, Iran: Portico of the "Hundred-columned
Hall" with colossal bull from the gateway

Pomegranate, Box 6099, Rohnert Park, CA 94927

Sifting the Sands of Time

Persepolis, Iran: Native workmen during restoration of
the Eastern Stairway of the Apadana, 1933

Pomegranate, Box 6099, Rohnert Park, CA 94927

Sifting the Sands of Time

Naqsh-i-Rustam, Iran: View of the Kaaba of Naqsh-i-
Rustam from a nearby cliff, 1939

Pomegranate, Box 6099, Rohnert Park, CA 94927

Sifting the Sands of Time

Tell Ta'yinat, Turkey: Surveying the excavation
around the double-lion column base, 1934–1935

Pomegranate, Box 6099, Rohnert Park, CA 94927

Sifting the Sands of Time

Luxor, Egypt: Members of the Epigraphic Survey
copy inscriptions and reliefs on the Bubastite Portal in
the temple of Amun at Karnak, c. 1935

Pomegranate, Box 6099, Rohnert Park, CA 94927

Sifting the Sands of Time

Abu Simbel, Egypt: The staff of the University of
Chicago Epigraphic Survey and young Charles
Breasted at the entrance of the Great Temple,
1905–1906

Pomegranate, Box 6099, Rohnert Park, CA 94927

Sifting the Sands of Time

Luxor, Egypt: Drs. Breasted, Nelson and Hölscher
examine the sarcophagus lid of Priest Harsiese,
Medinet Habu, 1928

Pomegranate, Box 6099, Rohnert Park, CA 94927

Sifting the Sands of Time

Kolba, Sudan: The University of Chicago caravan near
the Second Cataract, 1906

Pomegranate, Box 6099, Rohnert Park, CA 94927

Sifting the Sands of Time

Amara, Sudan: The University of Chicago caravan
leaving Amara, Nubia, 1906

Pomegranate, Box 6099, Rohnert Park, CA 94927

Sifting the Sands of Time

Tumbos, Sudan: Members of the University of
Chicago Expedition photographing inscriptions of
King Thutmose I, 1906–1907

Pomegranate, Box 6099, Rohnert Park, CA 94927

Sifting the Sands of Time

Gerf Hussein, Egypt: The forecourt of the temple of
Gerf Hussein, Nubia, 1905–1906

Pomegranate, Box 6099, Rohnert Park, CA 94927

Sifting the Sands of Time

Amada, Egypt: The Hypostyle Hall of the temple of
Amada, Nubia, 1905–1906

Pomegranate, Box 6099, Rohnert Park, CA 94927

Sifting the Sands of Time

Abu Simbel, Egypt: Excavating a stele to the north of
the Great Temple, 1905–1906

Pomegranate, Box 6099, Rohnert Park, CA 94927

Sifting the Sands of Time

Abu Simbel, Egypt: Interior of the Great Temple at
Abu Simbel, 1905–1906

Pomegranate, Box 6099, Rohnert Park, CA 94927

Sifting the Sands of Time

Abu Simbel, Egypt: Facade of the Great Temple, 1906

Pomegranate, Box 6099, Rohnert Park, CA 94927